CONTENTS

A MISSING RIVER

A group of scientists traveled to the Slims River in Canada in 2017. But when they arrived, the ground was mostly dry. The river was just a trickling stream. They hiked where the river was supposed to be flowing. Then they called a helicopter to pick them up. They flew upstream and found that the Slims River had been cut off from its water source.

The river used to get water from the nearby Kaskawulsh Glacier. The glacier would melt each spring. Water from it would flow into

Plants grow on the mostly dry riverbed of the Slims River.

Satellite images show the Slims River full of water in 2015, *left*, compared to 2016, *right*, when the water rerouted to the Kaskawulsh River.

the Slims River. The river flowed north into the Bering Sea. But in 2016, much more ice melted than usual. The additional water caused the land around the glacier to change shape. By late summer, water from the glacier went a different direction. It only flowed south into the Kaskawulsh River and to the Pacific Ocean. The change affected wildlife in many ways. Plants had less water. Animals had to move to find water. The Slims River fed Kluane Lake. The lake's water levels are now

Slims River →

Kaskawulsh Glacier ↓

Kaskawulsh River ↑

much lower. Climate change caused the rapid melting of the Kaskawulsh Glacier.

WHAT IS CLIMATE CHANGE?

Climate is the average weather of a certain place. Earth's climate is always changing. But in recent decades, its temperature has been rising. The top four warmest years on record were from 2015 to 2018.

Scientists have known since the 1960s that human activity has added greenhouse gases to the atmosphere.

CLIMATE CHANGE IS A BIG DEAL

Humans might not be able to feel Earth's average temperature changing. But climate change has a huge effect on nature. Dan Shugar was one of the scientists who discovered the missing Slims River in Canada. He pointed out that big changes are happening fast. "Nobody to our knowledge has documented [a large river reroute] happening in our lifetimes. . . . People had looked at the geological record—thousands or millions of years ago—not the 21st century, where it's happening under our noses."

Greenhouse gases get their name for how they trap heat around Earth like a glass greenhouse. Carbon dioxide, methane, and nitrous oxide are all greenhouse gases. Earth needs greenhouse gases to stay warm. But too much can raise Earth's temperature to levels that harm people and wildlife. There are many consequences of high temperatures, including habitat loss and stronger storms. Scientists are studying climate change to learn how to adapt to it and eventually stop it.

MAKING CLIMATE MODELS

One way to study the climate is to go somewhere that is strongly affected by it. Scientists often travel to these places to gather samples, take pictures, or observe ecosystems. But they also use technology to help them study climate change.

One of these technologies is a climate model. A climate model uses math equations. The equations predict how a change in the climate could affect the world's ocean, air, land, or ice. The models use a lot of information, such as air temperature and

HUMAN ACTIVITY CAUSING WARMING

Some human activity adds greenhouse gases to the air. Burning fossil fuels such as coal and oil creates carbon dioxide. Fossil fuels are often burned to power machines and cars. People drive cars every day. They work in factories or use machines daily too. In 2016 China and the United States each added more carbon dioxide to the air than any other country. In the United States, the biggest amounts of carbon dioxide were from electricity, transportation, and industry.

GREENHOUSE GASES IN THE
UNITED STATES

This pie chart shows the percentage of total US greenhouse gas emissions each sector contributed in 2017. Burning and producing fossil fuels such as coal, natural gas, and oil are some main ways greenhouse gases get into the atmosphere. Other main sources of greenhouse gases include industrial or farming practices as well as breaking down solid waste. How does knowing the main sources of some greenhouse gases help you understand how human activity affects the atmosphere?

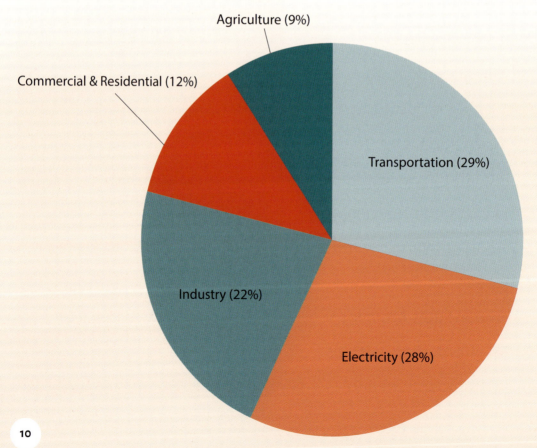

Agriculture (9%)

Commercial & Residential (12%)

Transportation (29%)

Industry (22%)

Electricity (28%)

the amount of rainfall. Climate models test possible solutions for future problems. Powerful computers calculate climate models.

Along with technology, scientists rely on nature to learn about climate change. They gather samples from the air, soil, water, and ice. The samples are evidence of past climates. Scientists study samples from nature to learn about what might happen to Earth as its climate changes rapidly.

EXPLORE ONLINE

Chapter One explains climate change. The article at the website below gives more information about climate change. What information is the same in both the chapter and the article? What information is different?

NATIONAL GEOGRAPHIC KIDS: CLIMATE CHANGE

abdocorelibrary.com/studying-climate-change

STUDYING AIR

Air may seem like it is empty. But it's made of gases. When scientists study air, they measure temperature, the amount of greenhouse gases, and water vapor. Water vapor is the gas form of water in the air. Water vapor is also called humidity.

Scientists collect air samples around the world. Sometimes they collect air from places far from human activity, such as at sea or in the desert. Samples from these areas show the most accurate data about the amount of

Clouds and fog are two visible forms of water in the air.

gases in the air. That is because they are not near buildings or human activity.

Scientists often use a special case to collect air samples. The case has two flasks in it. The flasks are connected to one end of a tube. The other end of the tube is run up a long pole. The pole extends up and out of the case. The higher the pole is, the purer a sample it can get. The sample will be less exposed to human breath or emissions from human activity. A pump pushes air into the flasks. It takes less than ten minutes to collect the samples. The flasks are sent to a lab. At the lab, machines measure the amount of different gases in each air sample.

Scientists collect air samples around the world, including in India.

SENSORS EVERYWHERE

Air sensors on tall towers also collect air samples. The sensors test the air directly and send data to computers. Sensors measure what makes up the air in a certain location. They can pick up temperature, humidity, and wind direction. They also track particles in the air, such as dust.

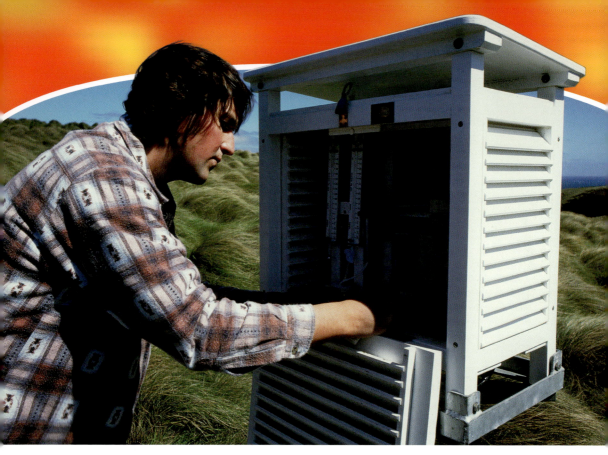

A case called a Stevenson screen allows air to flow to a thermometer while blocking direct sunlight.

Thermometers record temperature. Very precise thermometers measure air temperature with electricity. They are made of thin metal wires. The thermometers record how much electricity passes through the wires. The higher the temperature, the slower the electricity flows.

Some thermometers used by the US government measure the temperature every two seconds. They connect to a computer. The computer records the data. Every five minutes, it calculates the average temperature of the air in that location. The devices have a metal shield to block out sunlight. That way the thermometers measure only air temperature.

Recording air samples from the same place over time can show weather patterns such as wind direction. Scientists look for these patterns. Patterns may explain why the air in the location is clean or dirty. For example, high levels of pollution coming from the direction of a factory could be carried by the wind.

SATELLITES IN SPACE

NASA launched a satellite called Terra in 1999. It was still in use in 2019. Satellites orbit around Earth. They collect data about the atmosphere, clouds, the ocean, and land.

PERSPECTIVES

A NEW VIEW OF EARTH

Michael Abrams is a scientist with NASA. He was part of the team that worked on the Terra satellite. He believes satellites show a valuable new view of Earth. He said, "All our lives, we look from five feet up. . . . When we get really high, we gain an entirely different perspective of what our earth is and how it operates."

Terra has nine digital cameras to take pictures at different angles. It has sensors that measure the amount of greenhouse gases in the air. Terra's cameras helped scientists study smoke from California fires in 2018. Climate change can cause wildfires or make them worse. So scientists used Terra to learn more. They took pictures of the height, shape, and speed of the smoke. This information helped scientists predict how far the smoke would travel and whether or not they needed to warn people about breathing it in.

STRAIGHT TO THE
SOURCE

Josh Willis is a scientist for NASA. He studies climate change. Willis summarized the steps to researching climate change in a 2018 article:

> *The way science works is that I go out and study something, and maybe I collect data or write equations, or I run a big computer program. . . . And I use it to learn something about how the world works. . . .*
>
> *The weight of all of this information taken together points to the single consistent fact that humans and our activity are warming the planet.*

> Source: Holly Shaftel. "The Scientific Method and Climate Change." *NASA Global Climate Change*, 6 June 2018, climate.nasa.gov. Accessed 20 Nov. 2019.

BACK IT UP

The author of this passage is using evidence to support a point. Write a paragraph describing the point the author is making. Then write down two or three pieces of evidence the author uses to make the point.

EXAMINING SOIL

Scientists in Minnesota shove four metal stakes into the ground in a rectangular shape. The area is 150 feet (45 m) by 65 feet (20 m). The scientists spend hours identifying every plant species in this rectangle of prairie. A healthy prairie could have dozens of different species, from trees to mosses. This section of land is one of a planned 600 sites. Each site will be monitored every few years to see how it changes over time. Some changes could be caused by natural factors. Others may

Scientists in the Mediterranean region study plots of land to predict how climate change will affect plants.

PERSPECTIVES

PLANT GROWTH

Scientists expect that climate change will keep plants from reaching their full sizes. Hot tropical regions may lose growing days because of rising temperatures. Growing days are days when the temperature is right for plants to grow. Also, lack of water and changes in soil could limit the nutrients plants need to grow. Some cold places such as Russia, Canada, and China will gain growing days. But climate change will have a negative effect on plants overall. Camilo Mora wrote a study on how climate change would affect plant growth. He said, "Those that think climate change will benefit plants need to see the light."

be caused by climate change. The scientists mark the location with a GPS device. The metal stakes will help future researchers find the exact same location in several years.

Monitoring will let scientists see changes in the soil and everything living in it. Then they can compare the results of the study to other data about climate change, such as temperature changes in the region.

Monitoring will help scientists learn about the land so they can protect it.

SOIL SAMPLES

Scientists can learn about climate change from soil samples. Scientists collect some samples from varves. Varves are layers of silt and clay from the bottom of a body of water. Every year, soil, pollen, and more are washed into bodies of water. The material settles and gets covered by more silt. Over time, the layers build up and get packed down. Thick varve layers are a sign of heavy rains. Heavy rain washes a lot of material into the water. Thin varve layers are a sign of hot, dry years. Less soil would be washed into the water. From varves, scientists learn about ancient climates.

Another type of soil sample is permafrost. Permafrost is layers of water, soil, and rock that have been frozen for at least two years. Scientists must be careful when gathering these samples. Drilling a hole can create heat. This causes the ground to thaw.

Scientists can take soil samples using tools called augers.

Thawing can affect the temperature and moisture in the soil. So scientists blow cold air into the hole while drilling. This helps the ground stay its current temperature. Scientists use these samples to study how much of the ground stays frozen the whole year.

Scientists have found that more permafrost is thawing due to climate change. This thawing could add to climate change. Permafrost naturally stores carbon. When carbon is frozen, it is stored and kept out of the atmosphere. But when permafrost thaws, it releases carbon into the atmosphere. This adds even more greenhouse gases to the air.

SOIL STORES CARBON

Carbon is spread out on Earth. Some of it is found in the air and water. Some is stored in soil. Storage in soil is part of the carbon cycle. The carbon cycle is the process of carbon moving from one place to another. Scientists studying soil in Sweden found that climate change is affecting the carbon cycle. When the soil was wet, it was healthy. Tiny living things such as bacteria were active and moving. Bacteria broke down waste such as fallen leaves or animal poop. By breaking down waste, bacteria put nutrients, including carbon, into the soil. Plants use nutrients in the soil to grow. But in dry, unhealthy soil, the bacteria were much less active. Plant growth slowed. Scientists found that trees didn't take in as much carbon from the air. Less carbon was being moved to the soil. The carbon was still part of the air and part of the problem of climate change.

TREE RINGS

Studying tree rings helps scientists learn which climates are best for certain trees. Thick rings show good growing conditions such as enough water and the right temperatures. Thin rings show poor growing conditions, a lack of water, or natural disasters such as droughts or fires.

Scientists can count the rings to figure out in which year a ring formed. Then they look at weather records from that year. They can tell whether the climate conditions helped or hurt tree growth. For the future, scientists can use this knowledge to predict how today's warming climates may help or harm different types of trees.

The warming temperatures caused by climate change can dry out soil. Climate change can keep soil from taking in enough water. Since water is important for soil health, plant growth, and carbon storage, scientists are hoping bacteria can adapt to environments that are changing quickly.

STRAIGHT TO THE
SOURCE

Scientist John Firor worked for the National Center for Atmospheric Research. He explained how the ground's temperature helps scientists understand the surface temperature from long ago:

> One can find empty holes in the ground—abandoned oil wells, for instance—and put down a long line of thermometers. This allows measurement of the temperature of soil or rocks many levels down. The reason this works is because over time, the warmth at the surface is conducted to deeper levels. So, the temperature deep down in the hole relates to the surface temperature of long ago.

> Source: "Chapter 2: The Study of Climate Change." *Science Clarified*, 2020, scienceclarified.com. Accessed 2 Jan. 2020.

WHAT'S THE BIG IDEA?

Read the primary source text carefully. What is the main connection being made between deep holes and Earth's surface temperature? Explain how the main idea is supported by details, naming two or three of those details.

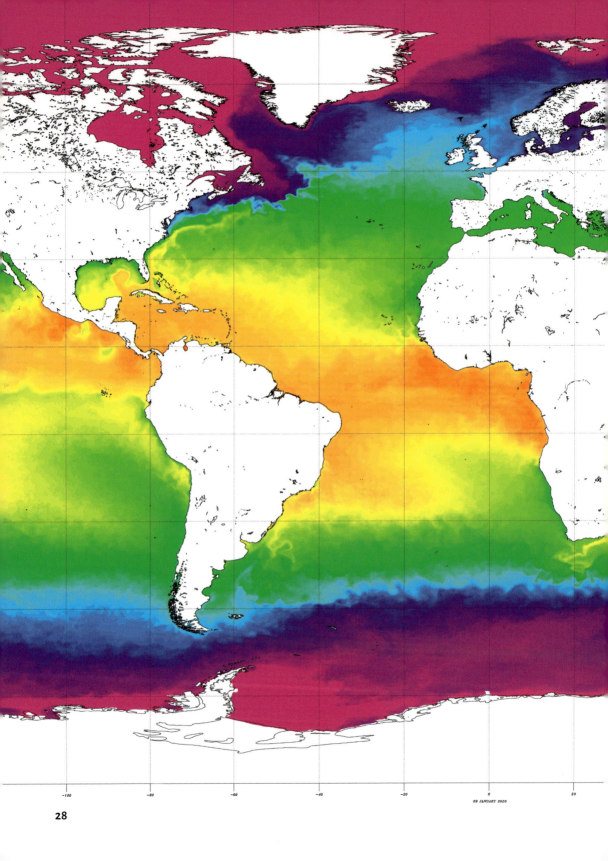

09 JANUARY 2020

INSPECTING WATER

Like temperatures in the air and soil, water temperature is measured often. Scientists can measure the surface temperature of the ocean in several ways. People on ships can stick a thermometer directly in the water. Thermometers can be attached to buoys. Buoys stay out in the water and take regular measurements. Sensors on satellites have become the most common way to measure surface water temperature.

Satellite information about sea surface temperature can be made into a map, where red and orange are hot and blue and purple are cold.

Scientists also measure precipitation. Precipitation is water that falls from the sky in various forms. Those forms include rain, snow, and hail. A rain gauge is one way to measure rainfall. This small container has an opening on top. As rain falls, it collects in the container. Marks on the container show how many inches or centimeters fell over a period of time.

PERSPECTIVES

WATER FLEAS

In 2018 scientists studied water fleas in lakes. These tiny creatures are related to shrimp. Many small fish eat water fleas. Larger fish eat those smaller fish. If climate change were harming water fleas, all other animals in a lake would be affected. The researchers saw that high levels of carbon dioxide kept water fleas from being able to defend themselves. Some kinds of water fleas have a crest on their heads to protect themselves. Others grow spikes. When there was too much carbon dioxide, they grew smaller crests and shorter spikes. Without a defense, they could die out.

NASA uses satellites including the Global Precipitation Measurement Mission Core Observatory to track precipitation.

UNDERWATER LABORATORY

The scientists at Aquarius study the ocean and coral reefs. Aquarius is a lab off the coast of Florida. It is 60 feet (18 m) underwater. Scientists live and work there for ten-day missions. The underwater lab saves time and money. Scientists can do short dives. They can dive deeper than they could from the surface. They study how climate change and pollution are hurting coral reefs.

Measuring the amount of rainfall is important for studying climate change. It helps scientists track changes in the weather. For example, heavy precipitation events are becoming more frequent in the United States because of climate change. By measuring precipitation, scientists saw trends of increased rainfall. These trends helped them predict that rainfall will become more frequent.

MEASURING SEA LEVELS

NASA satellites track sea levels. Sea levels have risen by 3.7 inches (9.5 cm) since 1993. Rising sea levels are a sign of climate change. Some ice on land and sea has been frozen for a very long time. As Earth's surface gets warmer, that ice melts. Melting land ice adds water to Earth's lakes, oceans, and rivers.

Sea ice usually reflects sunlight. This keeps the water cool. Melting sea ice exposes more water to the sun. When exposed, water absorbs energy from sunlight. Absorbing sunlight and energy further warms the water and can lead to higher temperatures and more ice melt. Additionally, as water particles warm, they expand. This can increase sea levels.

FURTHER EVIDENCE

Chapter Four talks about studying water. Identify the main point and some key supporting evidence. Then look at the website below. Find a quote that supports the chapter's main point. Does the quote support a piece of evidence already in the chapter? Or does it add a new piece of information?

NASA CLIMATE KIDS: WHAT IS HAPPENING IN THE OCEAN?

abdocorelibrary.com/studying-climate-change

TESTING ICE

Ice plays an important role in understanding climate change. Some glaciers have been frozen for hundreds of thousands of years. They show today's scientists what the climate was like before humans started adding greenhouse gases to the atmosphere. Scientists study ice cores from glaciers to learn how Earth's climate has changed over time. Evidence of past climates is frozen in ice. Evidence includes dust, air bubbles, sea salt, volcanic ash, and more. It can be frozen

Ice core samples often come from remote locations.

ARCTIC SEA
ICE MELT

These images show the minimum Arctic sea ice in 1979 and 2015. The minimum sea ice is the ice that is present all year. How do these images help you understand how Arctic ice is changing?

1979

2015

for many years. The deeper a sample is, the earlier a time period it is from. Ice cores come from ice sheets in Antarctica and Greenland. They also can be taken from glaciers on the tops of mountains.

Getting an ice core from Antarctica can be a long process. It can take six to eight weeks to get two ice cores that are 700 feet (200 m) long. The first step is choosing a spot to drill. Scientists look for flat, thick areas. Then they set up a tent and drilling machines. They start drilling. Some ice cores have been as long as 2 miles (3.2 km). Other ice cores can be drilled in less time. They're often just 3 feet (0.9 m) long. Both long and short cores are later cut into strips for testing.

DANGEROUS WORK

Drilling ice cores is dangerous. Researchers must battle extreme weather such as freezing temperatures and storms. Wildlife such as polar bears can be a threat. Researchers pack lots of supplies. Once they go out on a trek, help could be far away if they need it.

EVIDENCE INSIDE AN ICE CORE

Scientists study ice cores bit by bit. They melt or crush samples and run them through various machines. The machines detect bits of dust, volcanic ash, or a grain of sand. Scientists also notice pollution, forest fire soot, or bits of metal from rocks.

Bubbles trapped in ice cores tell about the atmosphere from when the core formed. To collect bubbles, the ice is first crushed under a vacuum hood. That machine keeps other air out. When the ice is crushed, the machine sucks the air from the ice into containers. Scientists then test the trapped air.

Evidence found in ice is tiny. Measurements must be precise. Scientists work in clean rooms. A clean room is a closed space with controlled air and temperature. Clean rooms are designed to keep out dirt and dust. In clean rooms, scientists wear gloves and body suits

Ice cores must be handled very carefully to avoid contamination.

to keep the samples pure. One fingerprint could ruin a sample.

RESULTS OF STUDYING ICE CORES

Scientists have been studying ice cores for decades. They have learned a lot. One major discovery was that the amount of carbon dioxide in the atmosphere is related to Earth's surface temperature. In other words, if carbon dioxide increases, temperature will follow.

Scientists use ice cores to track changes in temperature and gases in

Scientists study ice cores to learn about Earth's past climates.

the atmosphere. They can see how much ice melted the last time Earth's temperatures were as high as they are today. This information helps them determine how to handle rising temperatures. For example, they can warn people living on coasts about rising sea levels or flooding.

Studying climate change involves getting samples of water, air, soil, and ice. Scientists travel around the world and even use space technology to track Earth's climate. They aim to help people and wildlife survive by studying the planet's reactions to a changing climate.

FAST FACTS

- Climate change is the change in Earth's atmosphere over time. Humans are adding more greenhouse gases to the air. Greenhouse gases such as carbon dioxide and methane trap and store heat in Earth's atmosphere. They are necessary to keep Earth warm, but too much of them can cause problems. Rising levels of greenhouse gases are causing Earth's temperature to rise. This harms life on Earth.

- Scientists are studying climate change to understand how to adapt to it and how to stop it.

- One way to study climate change is to travel to certain locations. Scientists gather samples at these locations. They also rely on technology such as computers, machines, and satellites to help them study climate change from afar.

- Scientists take air samples to measure the amounts of gases and other particles in the air. They use thermometers to measure temperature.

- Scientists study soil and everything in it. They collect varves from the floors of bodies of water and permafrost from frozen ground. Soil samples can show changes in Earth's temperature as well as which living things survive best in different climates.

- Scientists use satellites and sensors to track water levels. They use rain gauges to measure rainfall.

- Scientists study evidence such as dust and air bubbles trapped in ice cores. They learn about past climates. One important discovery from studying ice cores was that the amount of carbon dioxide in the air is related to Earth's temperature. As the levels of carbon dioxide rise, so does the temperature.

STOP AND
THINK

Tell the Tale

Chapter One of this book discusses the experience a team of scientists had while studying the Slims River in Canada. Imagine you are making a similar journey to study a river. Write 200 words about how you felt when you found a mostly dry riverbed. How would you go about figuring out what happened to the river?

Surprise Me

Chapter Three discusses studying soil. After reading this book, what two or three facts about studying soil did you find most surprising? Write a few sentences about each fact. Why did you find each fact surprising?

Dig Deeper

After reading this book, what questions do you still have about studying climate change? With an adult's help, find a few reliable sources that can help you answer your questions. Write a paragraph about what you learned.

Say What?

Reading about climate change and the ways scientists study it can mean learning a lot of new vocabulary. Find five words in this book you've never heard before. Use a dictionary to find out what they mean. Then write the meanings in your own words, and use each word in a new sentence.

GLOSSARY

atmosphere
the layers of air around a planet such as Earth

conduct
to direct or pass on

flask
a container with a narrow neck and a cover or seal

glacier
a type of frozen water on land, formed over long periods of time by packed snow

GPS
the global positioning system, a technology that finds specific locations

orbit
to circle around another object

pollution
unhealthy particles or waste in an environment

satellite
a type of technology that orbits around a planet and gathers information

silt
fine particles of rock that are larger than clay but smaller than sand that settle on riverbeds or on the floor of other bodies of water

ONLINE RESOURCES

To learn more about studying climate change, visit our free resource websites below.

Visit **abdocorelibrary.com** or scan this QR code for free Common Core resources for teachers and students, including vetted activities, multimedia, and booklinks, for deeper subject comprehension.

Visit **abdobooklinks.com** or scan this QR code for free additional online weblinks for further learning. These links are routinely monitored and updated to provide the most current information available.

LEARN MORE

London, Martha. *The Effects of Climate Change.* Abdo Publishing, 2021.

Watts, Pam. *Ocean Ecosystems.* Abdo Publishing, 2016.

INDEX

About the Author

Emma Huddleston lives in the Twin Cities with her husband. She enjoys writing children's books about nature and animals. She thinks studying climate change is fascinating and important.